Dear Parents and Teachers,

In an easy-reader format, **My Readers** introduce classic stories to children who are learning to read. Favorite characters and time-tested tales are the basis for **My Readers**, which are available in three levels:

1 **Level One** is for the emergent reader and features repetitive language and word clues in the illustrations.

2 **Level Two** is for more advanced readers who still need support saying and understanding some words. Stories are longer with word clues in the illustrations.

3 **Level Three** is for independent, fluent readers who enjoy working out occasional unfamiliar words. The stories are longer and divided into chapters.

Encourage children to select books based on interests, not reading levels. Read aloud with children, showing them how to use the illustrations for clues. With adult guidance and rereading, children will eventually read the desired book on their own.

Here are some ways you might want to use this book with children:

- Talk about the title and the cover illustrations. Encourage the child to use these to predict what the story is about.
- Discuss the interior illustrations and try to piece together a story based on the pictures. Does the child want to change or adjust his first prediction?
- After children reread a story, suggest they retell or act out a favorite part.

My Readers will not only help children become readers, they will serve as an introduction to some of the finest classic children's books available today.

—LAURA ROBB
Educator and Reading Consultant

For activities and reading tips, visit myreadersonline.com.

For Vanessa

SQUARE
FISH

An Imprint of Macmillan Children's Publishing Group

MOLLY THE PONY. Text copyright © 2012 by Pam Kaster.
All rights reserved. Printed in China by South China
Printing Company Ltd., Dongguan City, Guangdong Province.
For information, address Square Fish, 175 Fifth Avenue, New York, NY 10010.

BREYER and BREYER logos are trademarks and/or registered trademarks
of Reeves International, Inc. Breyer's mission is to celebrate the horse
and create the world's finest model horses.

Photo credits: pp. 4, 28, and 29, © Dr. James Redmon; pp. 31 and 40, © Kaye Harris.

Library of Congress Cataloging-in-Publication Data
Kaster, Pam.
Molly the pony : a true story / by Pam Kaster ; adapted by Susan Bishay. — Revised/updated ed.
p.   cm.   — (My readers)

ISBN 978-1-250-00433-8 (hardcover)
1 3 5 7 9 10 8 6 4 2

ISBN 978-0-312-61121-7 (paperback)
1 3 5 7 9 10 8 6 4 2

1. Ponies—Anecdotes—Juvenile literature. I. Title.
SF315.K33 2012   636.1'6—dc23   2011030860

Book design by Patrick Collins/Elynn Cohen

Square Fish logo designed by Filomena Tuosto

Originally published: Louisiana State University Press, 2008
First MY READERS Edition: 2012

myreadersonline.com
mackids.com
breyerhorses.com

This is a Level 3 book

LEXILE: 560L

Molly the Pony

A True Story

by Pam Kaster
Adapted by Susan Bishay

SQUARE
FISH

Macmillan Children's Publishing Group
New York

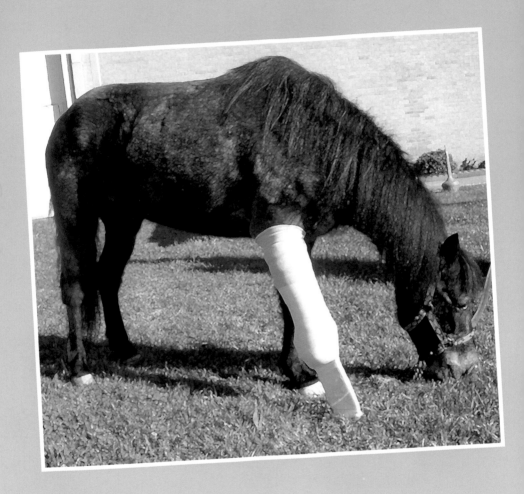

Contents

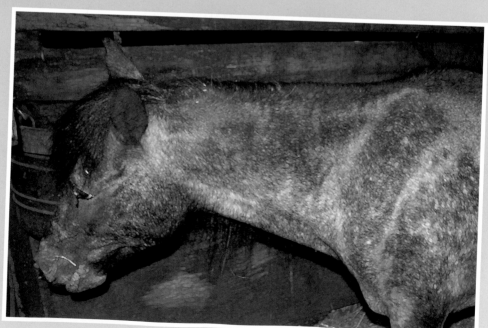

Chapter One

Hurricane Katrina

A storm was coming.

All day long, cars and trucks

filled with people and pets

drove away to safety.

By nighttime,

everyone was gone

except a small pony named Molly.

Molly was left alone in a barn.

She waited for someone

to take her away, too.

In the morning,

the sky filled with clouds.

The wind roared.

A huge tree fell on Molly's barn.

It rained and rained.

It rained so much

that water came into the barn.

Molly stood in a small space
in her stall to keep dry.

Finally, the rain stopped,

and the sun came out.

Molly found some hay to nibble,

and little puddles of water to drink.

Still, no one came for Molly.

She waited some more.

One morning,

Molly heard voices.

"A pony is trapped in there!"

one said.

"Are you sure?

It's been two weeks

since Hurricane Katrina!"

said another.

"The door is blocked by a tree.

We'll have to cut a hole

in the barn to get her out!"

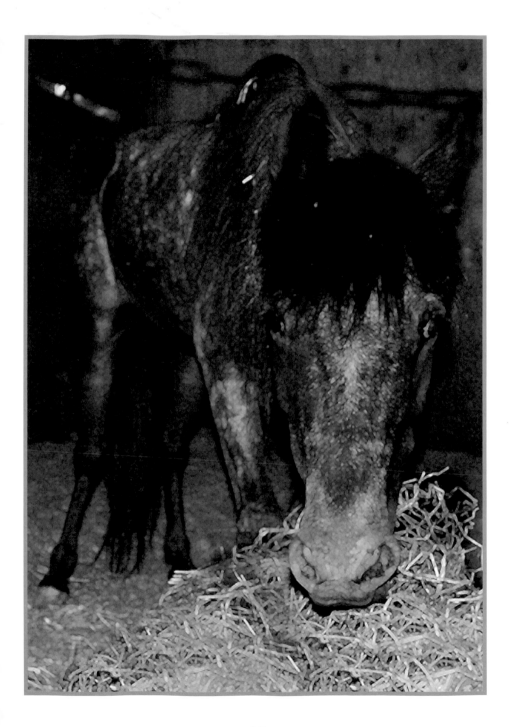

Soon, Molly was outside
in the sunshine.

"It's good your owners left hay
in your stall," someone said.
"They must have expected
to be away only a few days.
No one knew the hurricane
would cause so much damage."

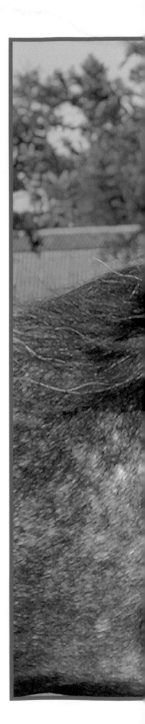

Molly was led to a trailer.

The trailer took her away

from the barn.

When the trailer stopped,
a lady led Molly into a small pasture.
"You can stay here on Ms. Kaye's farm
until your owners come to get you,"
she said.

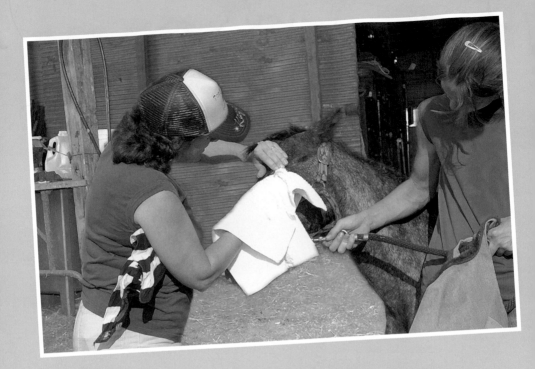

Chapter Two

A New Home

Ms. Kaye's farm had
lots of ponies and horses.
They became Molly's friends.
Ms. Kaye and her helpers
became Molly's friends, too.
They fed and groomed her
every day for three months.
One day, Ms. Kaye said,
"Molly, this is your home now.
Your owners said you can live here
with me and your new friends."

On a chilly winter day,

Molly stood dozing in the pasture.

Suddenly, a big dog

ran up and bit her.

Molly kicked out at the dog and fell,

but she could not make it go away.

Ms. Kaye chased the dog

out of the pasture.

But it was too late.

One of Molly's front legs
was badly hurt.
She couldn't stand on it.
Ms. Kaye cleaned and
bandaged the wound,
but Molly's leg didn't heal.
When a pony has
only one healthy front leg,
it's hard for the pony to get better.
The pony's healthy leg
has to do the work of *both* legs.
That can hurt the healthy leg.

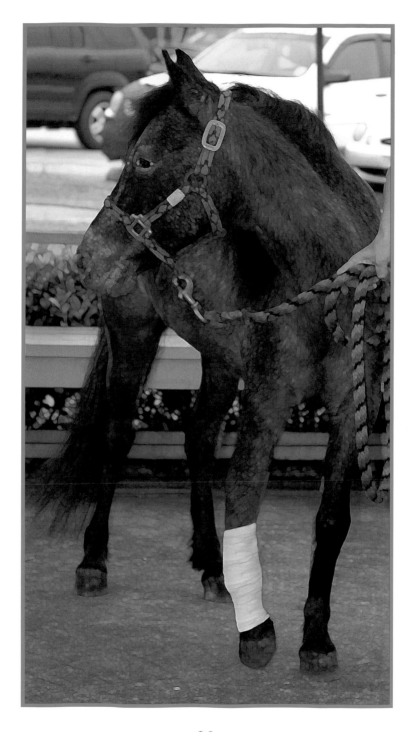

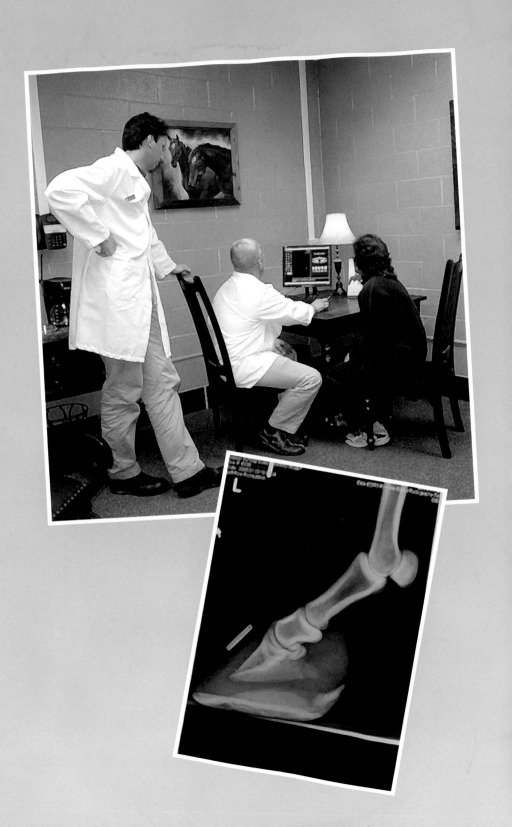

Chapter Three

Help for Molly

Ms. Kaye talked with animal doctors

called veterinarians, or vets.

At first, the vets didn't think

they could help Molly.

Then they watched her carefully

for a few days.

The vets were happy to see
that Molly knew how to rest
her healthy front foot.
"Molly is a smart pony
with a great attitude," said one vet.
"She knows how
to take care of herself.
I think she could learn to walk
with a prosthetic leg."
A prosthetic leg is made of metal.
It would replace Molly's injured leg.

At the animal hospital nearby,
the vets amputated
Molly's injured front leg.
They cut it off below her knee
and put on a stiff white cast.

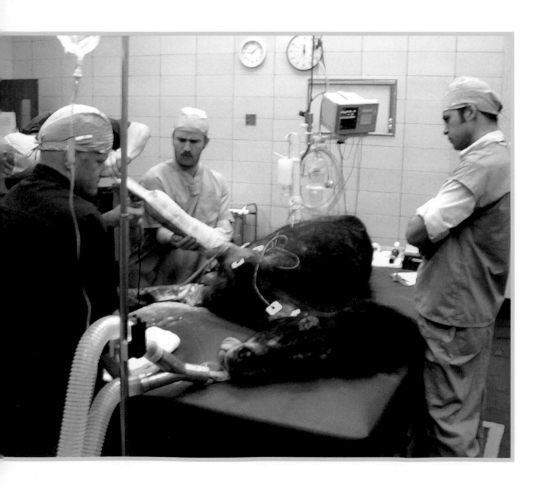

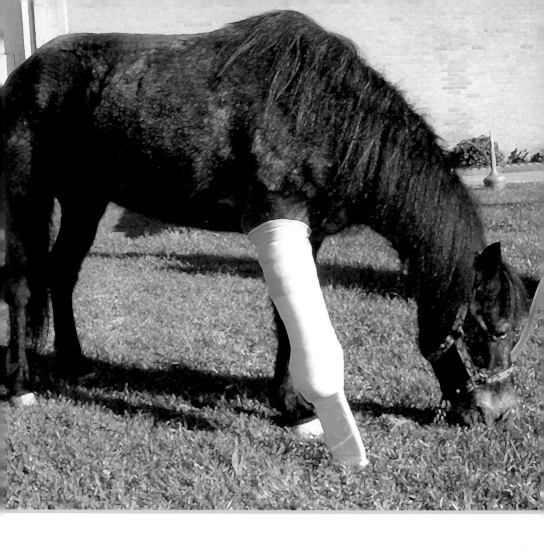

After four days
at the animal hospital,
Molly went home.

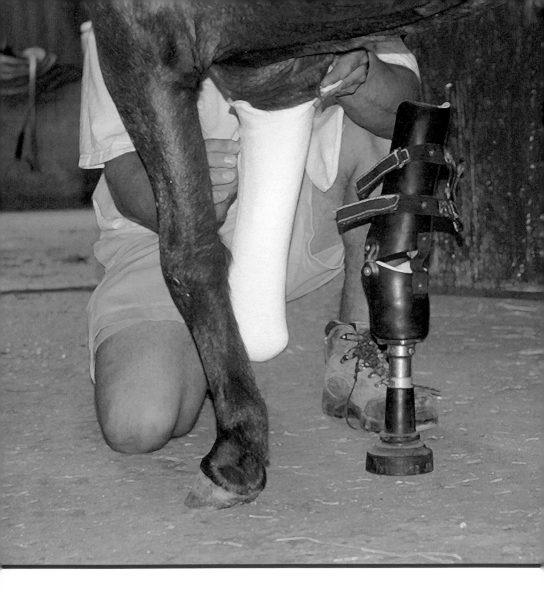

A month later,

Molly's cast came off.

It was replaced

with a prosthetic leg.

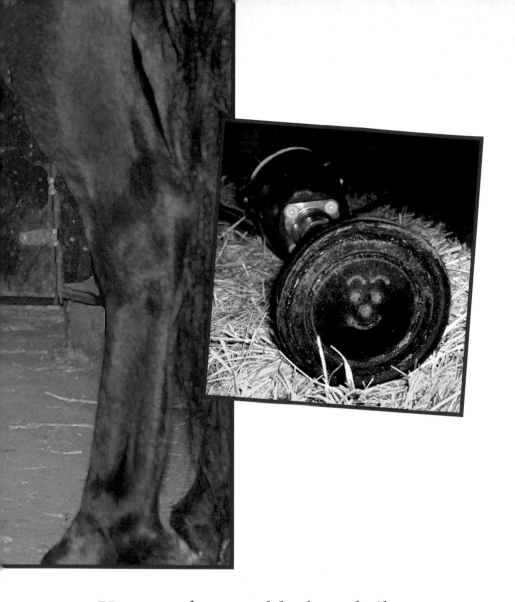

Her new leg was black and silver.

It had a round rubber hoof

with a smiley face

on the bottom.

At first,

Molly had a hard time

learning to walk on her new leg.

But the more she practiced,

the better she got.

Soon, she was trotting

everywhere.

Molly's farm friends were curious
about her new leg.
They touched it with their noses.
They saw that Molly was still
the friend they knew.

Now wherever Molly went,
she left a trail of hoofprints
with smiley faces.

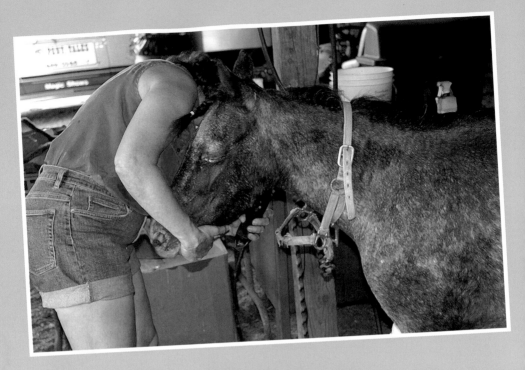

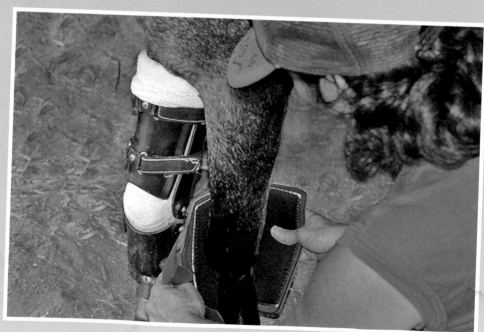

Chapter Four

Molly's New Job

One day, Molly started

a new job.

First, she got a good grooming.

An elastic wrap was placed

around her healthy front leg

to protect it.

Then, Molly climbed into her trailer

for a short ride.

When Molly arrived,

she stepped out of her trailer.

She wore a mask.

The mask kept the dust

out of Molly's eyes,

but she could still see through it.

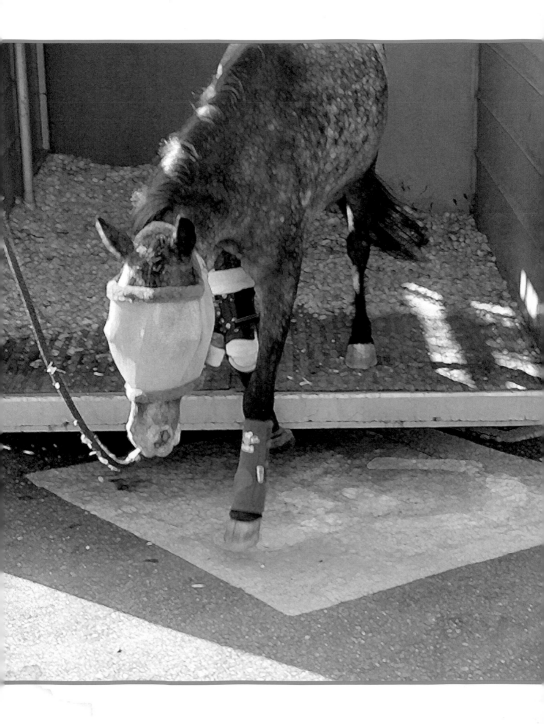

She visited a children's hospital.
The children were happy to see her
and to hear her amazing story.

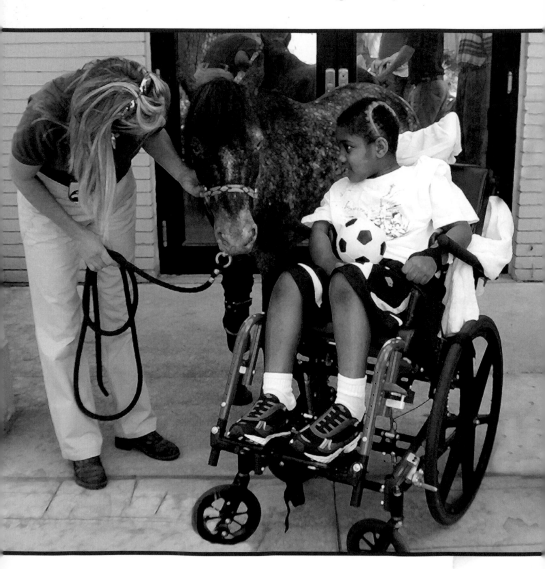

Then Molly visited
a retirement home.
The older people were happy
to see her, too.

Some of Molly's new friends
liked to pet her.
Some liked to touch her metal leg.
Molly stood quietly and gently
next to each of her new friends.

Molly's job was special.

She made new friends

and she made them happy.

At the end of her visit,

Molly stepped back into her trailer.

Ms. Kaye took her home

for a supper of oats and hay.

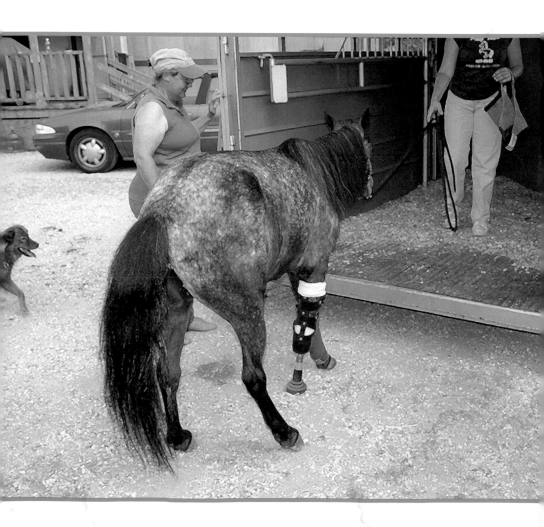

Wherever Molly goes,

she leaves a trail

of hoofprints

and smiling faces.

What a special pony!

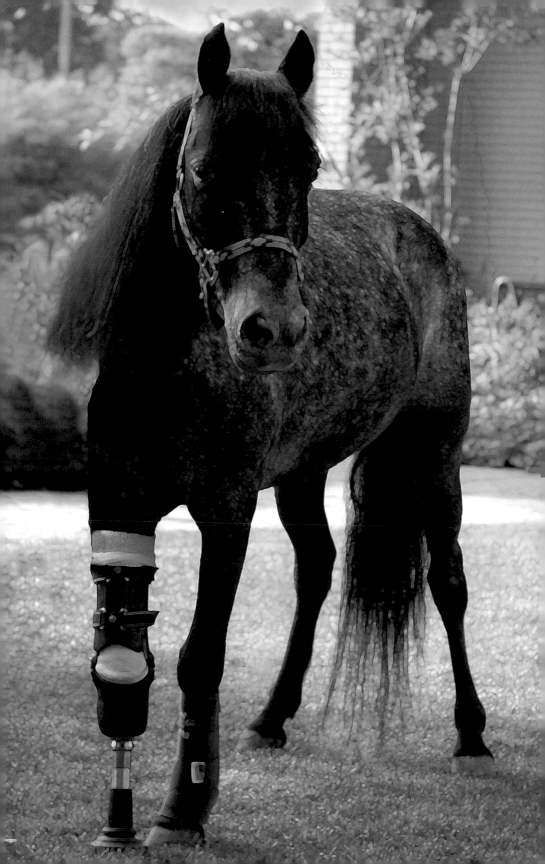

More About Molly

Molly is a small Pony of the Americas, a cross between a Shetland pony and an Appaloosa pony. She weighs approximately 410 pounds, and she stands about 44 inches tall at the shoulder. At the time of her rescue following Hurricane Katrina in 2005, Molly was eighteen years old.

During the first year after her surgery, Molly's prosthetic limb was redesigned three times to fit better. Each new leg always had a smiley face on its hoof.